St. Francis Of Assisi;

McIlvaine, James Hall, 1846-1921. [from old catalog]

ST. FRANCIS OF ASSISI

ST. FRANCIS of ASSISI

Six Addresses in Lent · By the Rev. J. H. McILVAINE, D.D.
CALVARY CHURCH · PITTSBURG, PA.

DODD, MEAD AND COMPANY
NEW YORK · MDCCCCII

UNIVERSITY PRESS · JOHN WILSON
AND SON · CAMBRIDGE, U. S. A.

TO

The Friends

IN WHOSE HOUSE THE WORK WAS DONE

THIS LITTLE BOOK IS DEDICATED

NOTE

THE writer desires to acknowledge his indebtedness in preparing these addresses to the works of M. Paul Sabatier, Canon Knox Little, Professor John Herkless, as well as to the earlier writers on the life of St. Francis.

CONTENTS

St. Francis of Assisi

I

THE MAN AND THE TIMES

THE lives of the saints are not attractive to us. They seem unreal, wanting in flesh and blood, a catalogue of impossible virtues, imbedded in a mass of legendary and incredible material. But they are not all of this character. In every age there are records of saints who were men of like passions with ourselves, but who were saints in this, that they heard and responded to God's call, they put God supremely and unmistakably first in their lives. We have a really human knowledge of Basil, Augustine, Gregory, Chrysostom, Catharine of Siena, Francis of Assisi, derived from their own letters, or the testimony of their cotemporaries.

We miss much of what is most worth having in life if we do not set apart a portion of our time to the study of the lives of the best in all generations. There we get what we can hardly get from any other form of literature; we see men as they actually were in the face of the common human temptations, trials, sorrows, that exist from age to age; how they prayed and struggled and suffered; how they dared to look forward and hope; and how, in spite of all, they, in a measure, triumphed. The reading is full of encouragement, for our minds become stored, like the scientific man's mind, with experiments, with the actual experience of Christian living; and it reinforces in us the sense that it is well worth while to be the best that we know. A man of profound moral insight has said: "When the best men cease trying the world drops backward like lead." When we look back on history we see how true that is. That which from time to time has raised the average level, which at all times keeps it from falling, is the influence of the best, those who have given all for all. They are the salt of the earth. The world half dislikes and is half afraid of them, but without knowing it is partly ashamed, partly encouraged, into rising a little way above what it would otherwise be. If we want to play our part in the world, to maintain the level from falling, and help it to rise a little, we can do it only by being the best that we know, obedient to the inner voice, true to the heavenly vision.

The lives of the saints are also of great value as a spiritual study, because they help us to accept God's will, and to gather fresh vigour for His glory. In such lives the truth is not merely written, it is seen in action. It is not easy to realise the truth of things; so it is helpful to study the actual lives of those who lived the truth. The teachings of Christ seem to us impractical and impossible until we see them acted out in a way that is marvellous, with a literalness that is startling, in the lives of men like, and yet so unlike, ourselves. We have drifted into the habit of half believing that the grace and power of Christ are confined to the New Testament, and that great sanctity is to be found only among His immediate followers. We measure things by the low standard of the customary and the commonplace, until there flashes upon us the high standard of the saints. Then in some measure we see and feel the greatness and the beauty of a true servant of God, and it makes us ashamed of our earthly views, our self-seeking ways, our often merely conventional religious forms.

I have chosen St. Francis as the subject of these lectures because he was pre-eminently the saint of the middle ages; and because, thanks to reliable documents, and the sifting work of historical criticism, we can get at the man behind the saint; we can see not merely noble actions, but life in its true meaning, and feel in him both the struggle and the development. How mistaken are those annals of the saints which represent them from the cradle surrounded with a halo, as if the noblest sight on earth were not that of a man conquering his own soul hour after hour, fighting against self, against suggestions of ease and idleness and pleasure, against unbelief and discouragement, and conquering at last through the grace of God!

St. Francis was also a great re-

former. He set himself to counter-
act the terrible evils before his eyes,
and to introduce a different spirit
into the life about him. He succeeded beyond all imagination, because of his method and spirit. He
embraced what would now appear
extreme forms of humility and
poverty, but it was what was needed
by his age. By his gentleness, courage, utter unselfishness, devoted love,
he alleviated the lot of the oppressed,
and exercised a vast influence in
undermining the principles which
made their condition unbearable.
He gave to the Christian religion
a new start, a fresh hold upon the
minds of men. In an age of practical irreligion, based on secret unbelief, the great nobles, as well as
the suffering poor, were awakened

to feel that a religion which produced such a life and teaching was a religion that men might still live and die by. He did an untold work for the saving of souls, for the advancement of religion, for the progress of civilisation, for the uplifting of society. If, as the centuries rolled on, his work seemed to fail, it was because his followers lost the spirit of their leader, and were untrue to the principles which he established.

He had apparently more than any other man whom we know in history what the Apostle Paul called the mind of Christ. " Let this mind be in you which was also in Christ Jesus, who . . . made himself of no reputation and took on him the form of a servant." His work in the world was accomplished through perhaps the closest following in the steps of the Master that the world has ever seen since the days of the Apostles. Like Christ he came " not to destroy, but to fulfil." He accepted the divine mission and authority of the Church, but threw a life and reality into what were fast becoming empty and lifeless forms. Like his Master he entered into closest sympathy and relation with the poor, the miserable, the lost. He sorrowed and suffered for men. He brought fresh hope into lives that were sinking in despair, and the sunlight of eternity into one of the darkest and stormiest days of time. His method was the method of Christ. With our colder hearts and worldly wisdom we may talk of him as eccentric and extravagant. What was Christ? The shallow and the scholar may both question his sanity. They called his Master mad. To save society Francis came into direct collision with society, as Christ had done before him. It was a fresh beginning, a reproduction in certain respects of the first age of the Church. He took Christ literally at His word, he believed that He meant what He said. The sermon on the Mount was to him the most literal of all directions. He felt that society needed arousing, reforming, saving, and that this could be done only by following closely, in his small way, the Master's lead. This is his strength and glory as a great reformer, that he more than any religious reformer since the Apostolic days had not only the genius to see, but the courage, the strength, the love to do what was needed for the great end before him. He more than any other — I say it after long and careful study of his life, and making full allowance for Roman exaggeration — followed exactly, literally, unflinchingly, in the steps of Christ.

To understand the significance of the life and work of St. Francis it is necessary to have some definite ideas of the state of Europe in the thirteenth century, to enter somewhat into the spirit, and know something of the religious and social conditions under which men lived; that we may realise the terrible need of some supreme man, who would set his back against the crying evils of his day, and not be afraid to lift his voice in denunciation of those in high places, yet would have all the kindness and sympathy and love for the fallen that a truly repentant sinner feels for his fellow sinners; that we may see in the person of St. Francis an instrument raised up by God for the purpose of setting before men the reality, the power, the joy of that religion which had become little more than a counterfeit.

"Mediævalism is the record of spiritual, mental, and political slavery; but it is also the fascinating story of the supremacy of the Church; of the Crusades with their forlorn hopes and splendid legends; of the piety that raised the Gothic cathedrals; of the universities with their weight of learning; of the friars, poor for Christ's sake; of the scholastics, justifying dogma; and the mystics, blessed with the vision of God. The mediæval Church policy meant just one thing, supremacy in things temporal and spiritual. For this policy Hildebrand was mainly responsible. In his strife with Henry, the stroke and counter-stroke were followed by the tragic scene at Canossa. With heavy step Henry climbed to the mountain fortress, for three days standing barefoot in the snow, clad in a coarse woollen shirt; he, the son of an emperor and himself the uncrowned Emperor of Rome, sought admission to Hildebrand, the son of the carpenter of Savona. When at last he was admitted to the presence of the Pope he threw himself on the ground crying, 'Spare me, Holy Father, spare

me!," Innocent III. who ascended
the papal throne in 1198, when
Francis was sixteen years old, was
a worthy successor of Hildebrand,
the strongest man in Europe. "In
the Empire he played the rivalry
of Otto of Brunswick against Philip
of Swabia, and changed German
history at will. In France he ap-
peared as the guardian of morality
and the Saviour of the oppressed.
Philip Augustus had put away his
Danish wife, Ingeburga, without
cause, and the French clergy had
granted the divorce. The queen
appealed to Rome. Pope Celestine
had quailed before the haughtiness
of Philip, but Innocent was a different man, and in him the king and
clergy found their master. Philip
was compelled to send away his be-

loved Agnes of Meran, and to take back his injured queen. In England King John had resigned his crown and received it back as a vassal of the Pope. In the East the Crusades had for the time seated a Latin king and established the Latin Church in Constantinople. The kings of Portugal and Aragon owned his sovereign power, which extended also over Bohemia, Hungary, and Poland." Throughout the civilised world the Church of Rome was supreme.

But the victory had been gained at the expense of religion. Every writer of the age stigmatises the dissoluteness of the clergy, and their scant regard for the common decencies of life. The traffic in ecclesiastical places was carried on with boundless audacity; benefices were put up to the highest bidder without shame. Innocent admits that fire and sword only could heal the plague. Prelates who declined to be bought were looked upon with wonder. Greed, cruelty, lust, polluted the lives of the Shepherds. Appeals to the ecclesiastical courts were constant against assassination, ravishment, incest, adultery. The number of bulls issued against these crimes among the clergy shows their prevalence. If the religious leaders were bad it is not strange that their followers were no better. The worst feature in this general decadence of morals was the callousness with which the worst forms of vice were regarded. Perjury, bloodshed, rapine prevailed, and public opinion acquiesced, raised no voice against it.

Superstition had taken the place of religion. Public worship had been reduced to a liturgical ceremonial which no longer appealed to the intelligence — a sort of self-acting magic formula. The pulpit, which ought to have shed some light, was silent; the Bishops alone were expected to preach, and they were absorbed in other matters. It was the work of Francis and Dominic, and the birth of the mendicant bodies that obliged the clergy to take up the practice of preaching. The worship of the saints under the guidance of an artful priesthood had loosened the bands of religion and lowered the standards of morality. Instead of high examples to be fol-

lowed, they were regarded as good-
natured intercessors to be bribed.
A man had only himself to blame if
he failed to secure their services. A
little attention paid to the saints,
with due liberality to their servants,
would save the most atrocious of-
fender. One of the legends generally accepted was that of a man whose
occupation was highway robbery.
He was taken and hanged, but while
the cord was about his neck he
prayed to the Virgin, and she sup-
ported his dangling feet with her
white hands for two days, and when
the executioner attempted to do with
the sword what the rope failed to
accomplish, the weapon was turned
aside by the same hand, until he was
compelled to release the criminal.
A parrot carried away by a hawk

uttered the words learned from its mistress, *Sancte Thoma, adjuva me*, and it was released. Relics were talismans which wrought cures even against the will of the sick. When the body of St. Martin was brought back to Touraine, two lame beggars who had gained a good living from their infirmity, were thrown into great fear lest they should be healed. They attempted to flee from the country, but on account of their lameness they had not reached the frontier when the body of the saint crossed it, and they were healed. Such stories were not received by the poor and ignorant alone; they were generally believed by all classes.

The feudal system was in full force. In the middle ages there were but two classes, the lords who owned the soil, and the serfs who went with it. The unsettlement of the Crusades, with the drain on human life, had impoverished the nobles, inclining them to be more stringent in their exactions, and adding to the sufferings, which under the best conditions, come into the lot of the labouring classes. Power was in the hands of a few, who used it largely for the oppression of the people. To no one in authority did the people seem of any account.

Italy in the thirteenth century was in almost constant warfare; its country districts depopulated; its fields protected only in the narrow circle of the garrison towns; the cities occupied in watching for the most favourable moment for falling upon and pillaging their neighbours; sieges

terminated by unspeakable atrocities
followed by terrible revenge; famine
accompanied by pestilence coming
in to complete the devastation. Nor
was this all. The wars between city
and city were complicated by civil
dissensions; plots were hatched
periodically, conspirators were exiled
or massacred if discovered; they
exiled or massacred others if tri-
umphant. Masses of human beings
were crowded together in squalor,
want, disease, and misery, left to rot
and die. " Society," says the late
Bishop of London, " was on the verge
of collapse when Francis of Assisi
stepped in and saved it." And again:
" The two men who have had the
greatest effect on modern history, in
widely different ways, are Napoleon
Bonaparte and Francis of Assisi."

St. Francis of Assisi

" In that iron age when brute force
was the main power and might was
right, the Church, with all its wounds,
with all its weaknesses, yet offers a
spectacle of moral grandeur, the
spectacle of a spiritual power commanding the rulers of the world, the
spectacle of peasants and labouring
men receiving the humble homage
of the highest potentates on earth
simply because, seated on the throne
of St. Peter, they represented moral
law.   What other conceivable power
or authority on earth would have
sufficed to tame savage and law-
less princes and barons, to restrain
in any degree the rapacity, greed, and
cruelty of men?   Things were bad
enough, it is impossible to justify the
methods used, but, all things consid-
ered, the papacy had a work to do in

the middle ages and it did it, imperfectly to be sure, but it did a work which, so far as we can see, no other power on earth, under the conditions and circumstances then existing, could have accomplished, — the work of saving the world from utter social and religious chaos."

For the Church was not all corrupt. Then as now the evil made more noise than the good. Here and there in the world there have always been souls capable of heroism if they can only see before them their true leader. St. Francis became for such in his day the guide they longed for, and whatever was best in the humanity of his time leaped to follow in his footsteps. A few great men, not the masses, have made the world what it is, and St.

St. Francis of Assisi

Francis was one of them. He profoundly influenced his own time, and his work follows after him; for all who contemplate his life are the better for it. To be good is the most and the best that a man can be, and goodness in another stirs the desire, and rouses the slumbering capacity for it in every heart that sees and knows it. Even a brief survey of such a life will help us, for on the one hand the weakness and shortcomings of his early life show us a man like ourselves, a poor sinner saved by divine grace; and on the other, the transcendent victories that he gained, and the wonderful results that he accomplished show us what a sinful man can become, what a sinful man can do, when, with a sense of his own weakness, reliance upon divine power sways his earthly life. Perhaps as we follow him in thought through these weeks of Lent, and see his self-sacrifice, his devotion to his Master, his intense love for souls, his great sorrow for sin, his patient resignation when all seemed broken and marred by failure, we shall receive into our own lives something of that which can be supplied from the truly beautiful and Christlike example of this Saint of God.

II

THE CONVERSION OF A SINNER

M. Paul Sabatier, the brilliant
French critic, has told us how he
came to devote so much of his life
to the study of St. Francis. He had
been to Assisi to see the place, and
was driving back to the station in an
omnibus. By his side sat a radical
free-thinking physician, who began
to talk with him about the saint. At
first he was sarcastic, asking if he
had any relics or wonder-working
articles of religion, which are the
principal object of so many visitors
to the shrine at Assisi. "No," M.

Sabatier said, " I have been looking chiefly at Giotto's work." It had hardly occurred to him that Francis himself was the main interest at Assisi, or that he was more than an ordinary saint of the Roman Church, a more or less legendary personage, with no particular message to this age, and no particular value to the world to-day. Then to his surprise the free-thinker burst out into most extravagant language of enthusiasm about St. Francis, speaking of him as one of the fathers of Italy, and one of the greatest reformers the world had ever known. This conversation was a kind of turning-point in Sabatier's life. His attention was arrested. Was this Francis of Assisi really all that men said? had such a man really lived in this world? He determined to find out for himself. The radical doctor deserves our thanks, for the conversion of Paul Sabatier to a belief in St. Francis has been the means of bringing home to people a far truer knowledge of the saint than was possible before the French scholar, a critic of the critics, began his patient and thorough investigations. M. Sabatier, in his life of St. Francis, has helped greatly to restore the portrait of the saint after its much retouching, by true critical and scientific methods, getting at the root of the story beneath the mass of legendary matter, and showing us what he really was to those who lived with him, and wherein lay the secret of his power.

There are few men who have not

cause to repeat with all the earnestness of their nature the words of the
Psalmist: " O remember not the sins
and offences of my youth, but according to thy mercy think thou
upon me, O Lord." The old
shadows cast their shadows still:
the old leaven may be purged away,
but the evil of its ever having been
there causes that hidden sorrow
which is both the pain of the peni-
tent sinner and the joy of the angels
over his repentance. So it was with
St. Francis. His story begins with
the sins of his youth, and they are
an ever present sorrow in his life.

Assisi is a little town lying about
half-way between Rome and Flor-
ence, somewhat to the east of the
ordinary line of travel. It was the
ancient Roman city Assisium where,

The Conversion of a Sinner

in the year 46 B. C. the poet Propertius was born.

" This city piled along the Umbrian hill
    Gave birth to two twelve hundred years apart,
    Who, handling the sweet mysteries of the
        heart,
    Sang both of love in measures memorable.
    Propertius tuned with less impassioned skill
    The strings which Ovid and Tibullus struck.
    He sang of woman, and of woe or luck,
    Determined, as it chanced, by Cynthia's will.
    And Francis, like Propertius, sang of Love,
    Love universal, utter and Divine,
    Love not of man or woman, but of all.
    All nations felt the quivering strings and
        strove,
    Till Love of Francis holds the world in thrall."

It is very much to-day what it was seven hundred years ago. The half-deserted streets, with their ancient houses, lie in terraces on the steep hillside. The feudal castle is there, but in ruins; the old Franciscan monastery on the brow of the hill, completed in 1228, is still inhabited by a few monks. The Church built at the saint's death is decorated by the frescoes of Giotto with twenty-eight scenes from his life. The houses crowded together climb up the narrow streets, their windows looking out on a panorama of the the wide Umbrian plain surrounded by green hills standing out against an azure sky. Here, in 1182, St. Francis was born. His father was Pietro Bernardone, a wealthy cloth-merchant. He was absent from home at the time of his son's birth, and his mother had him baptised John, but on his father's return he chose to call him Francis, the first use so far as we know of this name which has since been given in honour of him to so many kings and great ones.

The boy's education was not carried far. He knew the French language well; he learned a little Latin, and to write with difficulty. Throughout his life he used the pen rarely and but for few words; his autograph shows awkwardness, and he usually signs his letters with the mark of a cross. His father's wealth and possibly his mother's noble birth raised him to the level of the young nobility, and the money with which he was plentifully supplied, and which he liberally spent, made him welcome among them. He was too good-natured to refuse anything that was asked of him; too full of fun to be behind his companions in any mirth or festival or frivolity; too ambitious not to try to surpass them in every extravagance, and in not always innocent enjoyment. By his recklessness and wild pranks he became something of a celebrity in the town. He was constantly seen with his companions attracting attention by the richness of his dress and the noisiness of his behaviour. Even at night the revelling was kept up, making the town ring with their gay love-songs.

But even in these early years better traits of character appear. He was always courteous, polite, refined, generous, charitable. When he was asked for alms it was rarely in vain; if he had no money with him he gave some ornament or a part of his rich dress. Once, when in his father's shop, a beggar came in and asked for help in the name of God. Francis roughly sent him away, but immediately he reproached himself for his harshness, saying: " If he had asked something in the name of a count or baron what would I not have done? How much more when he asks in the name of God!" He ran after him and helped him.

When his school days were over he was associated with his father in business, where he showed that if he knew how to spend money he knew how to make it too; and gave his father great satisfaction by his ability. Associated as he was with the nobles, he was no mere man of fashion afraid of the sword, no hanger-on of rich men, but ever ready to defend the cause of the people. When war broke out between the people and their oppressors, the nobility, he took up the sword and fought with the people. The nobles, reinforced by the power of Perugia, were successful in a long and bloody engagement, in which Francis was taken prisoner. He was carried to Perugia, where he was confined in prison for a year, and where he astonished his fellow prisoners by his brightness and gaiety when others were depressed by their misfortunes.

When he returned he was twenty-two years old, and for several years seems to have continued in business with his father, but conducting himself in his old extravagant ways. Fêtes, games, festivals were in continual round. It was the age of the Troubadours. The movement caught the imagination of the young men, and especially that of Francis. He formed a kind of court. His personal charm and ample means gave him great opportunity. He was the leader among the young nobles at Assisi. He sang with them the songs of the Troubadours, conducted their processions through the streets, took the chief place at their banquets. He did his part so well that he became ill. For a long time he was laid aside, looking death in the face, and at this time the change in his life probably began. As he recovered strength the memories of the past came to him with great bitterness. He was dissatisfied with himself, his former ambitions seemed to him unworthy; he was learning that a life of pleasure leads only to satiety and self-contempt.

Yet knowing this he threw himself once more into the old round of pleasure-seeking, trying to divert his mind and forget his better thoughts.

An opportunity again offered of doing something as a soldier, and he hoped to find in military glory what he had sought vainly in pleasure. War had again broken out in Italy. A knight of Assisi was going to join the standard of Walter of Brienne, one of the most gallant leaders of the time, who was carrying all before him, and this knight offered to Francis the position of his esquire. He accepted with the greatest enthusiasm and delight. He made his preparations with great extravagance; his equipment was the talk of the town. He set out radiant with joy. But at Spoleto he was struck down

with fever. His companions went
on without him, and with them vanished his visions of military fame.
He returned to Assisi a disappointed
and discouraged man. He went
back to his old ways and his old
sins, but they had no longer any fascination for him, they left only a bitterness in his mouth. Disappointed
in pleasure and in glory, he turned
at last toward religion, as offering an
object worthy of the consecration of
his powers, and a satisfaction he had
not yet found.

Gradually a change took place.
One day he invited his friends to a
great banquet. Again he sat as king
of the revels, but with an absent look
on his face. One of the guests
taunted him with being in love, and
thinking of a bride. "Yes," he said,

" I am thinking of a bride more beautiful, more rich, more pure than you can possibly imagine." His bride was religion, or more likely the Lady Poverty, so styled in the sentiment of the times, whom Dante has wedded to his name. Giotto in one of the frescoes at Assisi has shown St. Francis placing a ring on the finger of a bride crowned with roses, but dressed in poor garments, with feet bruised by the stones and torn by briars.

His friends saw that he was in earnest and left him to himself. In a cave or grotto near Assisi he spent much of his time, mourning over his sins, praying for mercy, seeking truth and light; and the pallor of his face and the tension of his features told of the intensity within. One friend, different from

the others, probably the future
Brother Elias, was much with him,
helping and guiding him toward
the new life.

By degrees the struggle and
anguish passed, and calm returned
to his soul. Among the numerous
chapels near Assisi was one that
he particularly loved, that of St.
Damian. There was nothing in it
but a simple stone altar and a cruci-
fix over it. One day he was praying before the altar with his eyes
fixed on the face of Jesus on the
cross. It looked down on him with
an expression of infinite pity and
love. It seemed to say, "Come unto
me." He could not withdraw his
eyes; the figure seemed to be alive,
and through the silence he became
aware of a voice speaking to him

tenderly from the cross: "I have accepted thy sacrifice, thy desires, thy offering, thy work, thy life, thyself." His heart henceforth was filled with peace and his life with power. Whatever we may think of this occurrence which is related by all his biographers, it is quite certain that to St. Francis himself it was real, and that it had a profound effect upon his life. Until then religion had been for him a mere form, a meaningless ceremonial. For the first time he was brought into personal relation with Jesus Christ. The look of love cast upon him from the cross was never to pass from his memory. His only question henceforth was what did Jesus want him to do. He believed himself called of God. To those who believe in the call of Samuel there is nothing incredible in this. God is always calling us. The very word Church, *ecclesia*, means those who are called of God. "For ye see your calling, brethren," says the apostle; "how that not many wise men after the flesh, not many mighty, not many noble, are called." The saint is one who recognises the call of God and responds with complete self-surrender.

When Francis turned toward religion it was with his whole heart, with all the ardour of his impetuous nature. He could not be half-hearted in anything. What he did, he did with his might. God can do much with such natures. The world has great need of them. For them there is a peace, a joy, a fulness of power that the half-hearted can never know. Francis found in Christ and the service of Christ the satisfaction that he had sought vainly in the pleasures and pursuits of the world. With all his trials and sufferings and renunciations he was a happy man, his life was a happy life. No one can read it without feeling that gladness is its predominating note. He had found his true Master, "whose service is perfect freedom;" he had found the meaning of his life, and his face was set steadfastly toward the goal. The trouble with most of us is that we are half-hearted; we are trying to serve two masters; our hearts are distracted by the claims of God and the cares of the world; our lives divided into two sections, one given to God and the other kept for self, and there

is constant friction and disappointment and failure. Oh, to have a
vision of the highest and best and to
surrender unreservedly to it, think
what it means. It means something
of pain perhaps, something of sacrifice surely, but it means also to have
the heavens opened and to see Him
who is invisible; to have fellowship
with God through Jesus Christ His
Son; to have a guide in every choice
of life, a clue in every labyrinth of
duty, a joy in every sorrow, sunlight in the misty morning, songs in
the night. For such there is a peace
that the world cannot give, a power
the world cannot resist, growth in all
that stretches heavenward, complete
assimilation at last to the likeness of
Him who is loved and served.

III

THE MAKING OF A SAINT

THE vision at St. Damian's was the crisis in the conversion of Francis. From that time the Lord Jesus Christ was a real, living person always present to him, known and loved by him. Henceforth he was a Christian, Christ's man, seeking only to know and do his Master's will. He did not give himself to a life of seclusion and contemplation according to the custom of the day. He felt that activity called him, that his faith demanded works, not words, as its expression. He did not wait for great things, but accepted the work, however humble, that was nearest to him, that needed most to be done. As he rose from his knees and looked about him, the first thing that caught his eye was the dilapidated condition of the little chapel which had been to him a kind of Bethel. He seemed to hear a voice saying, " Go restore my house that is falling into ruins." As he came out he gave to the priest all the money that he had. His horse and a few pieces of cloth were now his only possessions. These he sold, and laid the money on the altar. He went into the open squares of the city and told those who gathered about him of his intention, and begged their help. Some laughed at him, but others were touched, remembering the brilliant youth. He took the stones that were given him on his shoulders, little used to such heavy work, carried them up the hill, and laid them with his own hands. As he had nothing to eat, and no means, he was compelled to beg his bread from door to door. It was not an easy task. The first time he looked at the broken, repulsive food he had received, he could not touch it, but each hour brought him strength. One day when begging for St. Damian's he passed a house where a banquet of his former companions was going on. At the sound of their well-known voices the memories of the past came back to him, and he could not enter, but turned away. Then, disgusted at his own cowardice, he returned, entered the hall, and after confessing his shame, pleaded with so much earnestness for his work that they could not help contributing.

The poor, to whom he had always been kind and charitable, now became his constant care. He was filled with the thought, not uncommon to the piety of the middle ages, that they were the representatives of Christ, "who though he was rich, yet for our sakes became poor." He loved their simplicity, their gratitude, their kindness to one another, their contrast to the ostentatious selfish pride of the rich. He studied so deeply the character of the Lord that he felt a great enthusiasm for poverty. To have complete control of himself, to give up all that hindered him from doing the perfect will of God, was his great desire.

Some time before this he had made a pilgrimage to Rome, where he saw with pained surprise the selfish extravagance and waste, and the meagre offerings to religion. He emptied his purse and laid all that he had on the altar at St. Peter's. He knew little as yet of the humiliations and pains of poverty. He loved fine clothes and dainty food. He desired to know what it would be like to wear coarse, soiled garments, to have nothing to eat, and to depend on the charity of others. He borrowed the rags from a beggar and stood for a whole day in the piazza of St. Peter's, fasting, with outstretched hands. It was a hard struggle and a great victory over his natural pride.

St. Francis of Assisi

Returning to Assisi, a more difficult trial awaited him. As he was
riding one day, at a turn of the road
he found himself face to face with a
leper. The awful sight had always
caused him horror and loathing. By
an instinctive movement he turned
his horse in another direction — but
only for a moment. Remembering
his Lord's example he conquered his
revulsion, sprang from his horse,
gave the poor wretch what money
he had, and when he left him stooped
and kissed his hand. A few days
later he went into a lazaretto and for
some time devoted himself to the
care of these unfortunate beings.

Few persons in the world were
more utterly miserable than the
lepers of that time. Like living
corpses, in gray garments reaching

to their feet, with hoods over their faces, they went about carrying a large rattle, St. Lazarus' rattle it was called, to give notice of their approach. From the prevailing conditions of filth and the absence of all sanitary regulations, the disease had spread through Europe like a scourge. Medical science was powerless against it. They were herded together like animals and left to die, with no one to tend to their bodies and none to care for their souls. There had been One in the world once who did not shrink from them, who laid His hands on them, and said, "I will, be thou clean." St. Francis required no other example than that of his Master, in whose steps he was learning to follow. Just because they were miserable, forsaken, helpless, this fastidious and sensitive young man, in the greatness of his love, gave himself for their help. Overcoming his natural loathing, he not only tended, nursed, comforted them, but he showed them the warm affection which he really felt; he washed their feet, dressed their sores, ate at the same table, and even kissed them. Disgusting and loathsome, we think; yes, and disgusting and loathsome to him too, but if he thought it was what Christ wanted, the more loathsome it was the more lovely it becomes. In his last will and testament, one of the few authentic documents that we have from his hand, he writes: "When I was in the bonds of sin it was bitter and loathsome to me to look upon persons infected with leprosy, but that blessed Lord brought me among them, and I did mercy with them, and when I departed from them what seemed bitter and loathsome was changed to me into great sweetness and comfort both of body and soul."

Nor was his work for them merely the enthusiasm of love. There was in it a far-reaching wisdom. His sacrifice was not without lasting results. What he did for the lepers himself he made a part of the rule of the Order which he afterwards founded. Men of all ranks entered the Order, men of culture, of wealth, of noble birth, but whoever they were, they had to spend a part of their time in the hospital tending the lepers. From this two things followed, one, an improvement in the sanitation of the towns and proper treatment of the disease, by which in the course of time the scourge was completely eradicated from Europe: the other, an impression on the world, which could not otherwise have been made, of the reality of the love and religion which inspired these men.

Another trial was the anger of his father and the severance of his family ties. Bernardone, the proud and successful man of the world, was disgusted with what seemed to him his son's infatuation. He was willing to provide money for his dissipations, but not for his charities. One day as Francis passed through the streets, pale, emaciated, his garments torn and soiled, he was greeted with the shout *Un pazzo!* A madman!

The Making of a Saint

There is an old Italian proverb *Un pazzo ne fa cento* — One madman makes a hundred, and quickly an excited crowd gathered about him throwing sticks and mud. Bernardone heard the clamour and went out to enjoy the sight, when he heard his own name, and perceived his son the object of so much unpleasant attention. Filled with shame and rage he seized him, dragged him home, and when threats and bad usage failed to change him, had him cast into prison and appealed to the magistrate. Francis claimed, as a servant of the Church, exemption from civil jurisdiction, and was sent to the Bishop for trial. The Bishop refused to interfere, advising Francis simply to give up all his property. Instead of replying

57

he retired to another room of the
palace, and soon returned holding
in his hand a package in which he
had folded the clothes he had on,
and on which he placed the little
money that he had. These he laid
down before Bernardone. " Listen all
of you," he said. " Until this time I
have called Pietro Bernardone my
father; now I desire to serve God.
This is why I return this money,
for which he has given himself so
much trouble, as well as my clothing
and all I have had from him, for
henceforth I desire to say nothing
else than ' Our Father who art in
Heaven.'" Bernardone took the
clothing, and the Bishop had to
give Francis an old mantle to cover
his nakedness. Henceforth you will
notice nothing more is ever heard

of the rich, worldly-wise, self-seeking Bernardone, save as the father of the son whom he cast off in contempt. The prudent, practical, common-sense merchant, is dead and forgotten these seven hundred years. Francis, his son, acts on the principles of Christ, accepts the wisdom of God which is foolishness to the world, and his name lives and will live so long as there is a sense of greatness and goodness in the world and vitality in the Christian faith.

Leaving the palace, Francis went out into the streets, thence into the forest, clothed only in the mantle the Bishop had given him, singing one of those Troubadour songs of chivalry he had learned in days gone by. Some robbers aroused by his sing-

59

ing, seized him. "Who are you?"
they demanded. "A herald of the
great king," Francis answered; "but
what is that to you?" They stripped
him of his only garment and threw
him into a ditch full of snow. "Lie
there, poor herald," they said; "that
is the place for you." He made his
way, stiff with cold, to a monastery
near by, and offered to make himself useful to the monks in any way
they might desire. They set him to
work in the kitchen, but gave him
nothing to cover himself with, and
hardly anything to eat. He went
back to his friends the lepers, who
received him gladly, comforted his
heart with their affection, and from
their scanty stores gave him what
he needed. Soon after we find him
at St. Damian's, where he completed

the work of restoration which he had begun before. Then he set himself in the same way to restore two other churches that sadly needed repair. One was San Pietro near Assisi, the other, afterwards so closely connected with his name, was S. Maria degli Angeli, usually called St. Mary of the Portiuncula, which became a kind of home for the outcast and was always very dear to his heart.

Here on the feast of St. Mathias in February, 1209, when he was twenty-seven years old, Mass was being said. When the priest turned to read the Gospel for the Day, Francis felt the same strange, overpowering sensation which had come to him three years before at St. Damian's. He no longer saw the priest;

it seemed to him that it was Jesus who was speaking, and speaking directly to him. The words read were these: " And as ye go preach, saying, The kingdom of heaven is at hand. Heal the sick, cleanse the lepers, cast out devils; freely ye have received, freely give. Provide neither gold nor silver nor brass in your purses, neither two coats, neither shoes, nor yet staves, for the workman is worthy of his meat." (Matt. x. 7–10.)

They were the words he had been waiting for. They came to him like a revelation from Heaven. He accepted them literally, not trying to explain them away, not saying they were meant for other conditions of life and were impossible for him. He took Christ at his word without reservation or limitation. " As ye go preach " — " provide neither gold nor silver nor brass in your purses " — henceforth preaching and poverty were the watchwords of his life. He threw away his stick, his wallet, his shoes, determined to obey implicitly, without questioning, the commands of Him whom he had taken as his Master and Lord.

The next day he began to preach at Assisi with great simplicity, but great power. His preaching was chiefly the need of repentance, the blessedness of forgiveness, the sweetness of Christ's love, the glory of trying to follow His perfect life. The words came from the heart and went to the hearts of those who heard them. It is easy for men to escape the power of one who speaks from the pulpit. It is his business to preach, he belongs to a class set apart for that purpose. It is not so easy to escape the power of one who walks by their side, a layman like themselves, whose own life is an illustration and example of his preaching. Francis had given himself so completely that he had a right to claim renunciation of self from others. His person and life were themselves the sermon; he spoke only out of his own experience, asking others to do as he had done that they might find the joy that he had found. From that day he was a man of power. The voice of one who had given up all for Christ moved Assisi, moved the century, still moves the world.

Poverty to St. Francis was no giving up of property merely as an act of self-denial; no fanatical stripping of himself for eccentricity and notoriety; no price paid here to purchase Heaven hereafter. It was to him a means of freedom, that he might follow Christ more perfectly. He recognised the mistake of the rich young man in the Gospels. He saw that he was fettered by his wealth, that Christ wanted to make him free, to make him rich, to give him what he lacked, but the sacrifice was too great, and he went away sorrowful. St. Francis was what this young man might have become if he had not made "the great refusal." Poverty was not hardship to him, but happiness. In giving up all he found that he had gained all. He was no more bound down by earthly cares; he was free from the worries and anxieties of the covetous man whose unfilled desire is ever to have and to get; he revelled in the sunlight of God's presence, desiring only to have what God chose to give him, and to be what God would make him. He was like the lily that drinks in the dew and the sunshine, and is simply the lovely thing God would have it be. Here is the secret of his love for Nature. The beasts, the birds, the flowers, the water and fire, the sun and moon were his brothers and sisters, poor like himself yet rich, with nothing between them and heaven, doing God's will, living by God's power and to His glory. There is a vein of sunshine running all through his life. Though never a soul was more filled with penitential sorrow, he was yet bright as a spring morning. Francis the saint was still Francis the young cavalier, full of song and fun as in the old days. He has his little jokes with the brothers, plays with them, will not allow any sour looks about him, tells them to look happy even if they feel like crying. *Il avait un cœur toujours en fête.* He was always keeping festival. No one had more of disappointment, annoyance, trial, to go through, but he was to all who came near him a power of brightness, making them feel the exhilaration, the sweetness, the poetry, the comfort, the glory of trying truly to follow Christ. "Sweet Saint Francis of Assisi," sighs Lord Tennyson, "would that he were here again."

IV

THE LABOURS OF AN APOSTLE

THE ideal of St. Francis was none other than that of Jesus Christ. He tried to look at life from the standpoint of Christ; to be to the world, in his measure and limitations, what Christ had been. Absolute self-renunciation was indispensable to a true and faithful following of Christ. The perfect Master had not where to lay his head, why should the sinful servant have more? True to his ideal he gave up all that he had, and became, in his own language, *Il poverello* — the little poor man. He adopted the brown woollen gown tied with a rope, which the poorest men of the time wore, and he went bare-foot as they did.

He had as yet no thought of founding an Order. He simply de-sired men to follow Christ, and he tried to show them how he thought they ought to do so. But such a life inspires imitation. There is a yearn-ing in the human heart for complete devotion. The scoffing of the early days had given place to admiration. Renan says: "The great Umbrian movement of the thirteenth century is, among all attempts made at a great religious foundation, the one that most resembles the movement in Galilee." One after another there was gathered about him a little body of disciples. The first to come was

The Labours of an Apostle

Bernard Quintavalle, a citizen of Assisi, and a man of wealth and prominence. He had been greatly impressed by the sincerity, patience, and devotion of the young man. He had several times given him shelter in his house. On one occasion, when they were sleeping in the same room, he had seen Francis get out of bed, and going down on his knees, repeat again and again, the tears streaming down his face, *Deus meus et omnia,* — My God and my all. Soon after he, and a Canon of the Church of St. Nicholas named Peter, sold all that they had, gave the proceeds to the poor, and joined Francis. They built a little hut for their shelter. This was in April, 1209. A week later came another disciple, Egidio, like Nathanael, " an Israelite indeed,

in whom was no guile," a pure and
beautiful soul, a true and knightly
spirit, whom Francis used to call the
knight of their Round Table.

With these three companions he
set out on his first missionary journey, going two by two, Bernard and
Peter, Francis and Egidio. They
went up and down the country,
preaching repentance and self-renunciation, sleeping in hay-lofts, the
porches of churches, or the leper
hospitals, working by day in the
fields for their bread. Their strange
costume, their brightness and happiness and fearlessness, the simplicity
of their words, attracted people.
Some thought them mad, others felt
that there was more than madness in
their action. The result was not
great, but a beginning had been

made. They returned to Assisi, where they were joined by four others, of whom we know little more than their names.

Portiuncula, "the little portal," where Francis had first heard the words that called him, was their place of meeting, for they had no house or home. They went about the country preaching, working for their living when they were able, often in want, sometimes nearly starving, but always joyous. The Bishop of Assisi said to them: "Your way of living without owning anything seems to me harsh and difficult." St. Francis answered: " If we possessed property we should have need of weapons to defend it, for it is a source of quarrels and lawsuits, an obstacle to the love of God and our neighbour." He saw that the whole feudal system, with its endless warfare and oppression, rested on the possession of land and property. For this everything else was sacrificed. What was needed above everything else was the example of a life not dependent upon what the rest of the world craved, and for which they were selling themselves. He felt that society needed something like a shock to rouse and reform it, and that nothing but a life of absolute poverty could reach the luxury and selfishness of the times. They met much opposition from the clergy, to whose avarice their poverty was a rebuke; and from the families of the rich and powerful, who feared that their sons might be drawn to imitate such insanity. They were often attacked and insulted; sometimes their clothes were torn from them and they were covered with mud and filth. Their only answer was, " God forgive you."

The number of the little band had now increased to twelve, and Francis felt that the approval of the Pope was necessary to the movement. Full of hope the little company set out for Rome. The Bishop of Assisi happened to be in Rome when they arrived, and through his services an interview with the Pope was obtained.

Innocent was then engaged in the great ecclesiastical movement for supremacy which Hildebrand had begun. The Vicar of Christ could not be superior to emperors and kings unless he surpassed them in pomp and magnificence, and the striving for worldly splendour had infected the whole ecclesiastical system. In one of the frescoes at Assisi, Giotto has represented this interview of so much dramatic and historic significance. Innocent seated on his throne looks with wonder in his eyes on the strangers, clad in peasant clothes, torn and stained and footsore with their long journey, asking nothing, claiming no privilege, save the privilege of following Christ, and of absolute conformity to the teachings of the Gospel. The Pope could not approve of them without condemning himself and the whole aim and ambition of his life; he could not condemn them without denying the teaching and commands of Him whose vicar and representative he claimed to be. So he neither approved nor condemned. He gave them kind words, he authorised them to continue their work under the consent of the Bishops; he required them to accept the tonsure which marked them as no longer laymen, but belonging to one of the minor orders of the clergy; and from this time they were under the authority and supervision of the Church. This is the turning-point of the whole movement, the tragedy of St. Francis' life. It was the giving up of his liberty and the entering into bonds that never ceased to burden him, and against which he protested to his latest sigh. Never did man hear more clearly the voice of Christ, but he thought that obedience required

submission to one whom he regarded as the Vicar of Christ, and
in perfect humility and obedience
he surrendered. Henceforth the
struggle was between the Franciscan ideal, sublime, unworldly, Christlike, and the ecclesiastical policy of
the time, until Francis, defeated,
heartsick, feeling that his great ideal
had been spoiled and taken from
him, abdicated the direction of his
spiritual family, and under his successors we see the triumph of the
ecelesiastical idea, and the whole
of the great Franciscan movement
turned into a subtle engine of spiritual domination and material aggran-
disement. That was the tragedy of
St. Francis.

They returned to Assisi preaching by the way. About an hour's

walk from the town was a ruined, deserted cottage, formerly a resort of lepers. It was so small that there was hardly space for them to live, but here they took up their abode, visiting and preaching in the neighbouring towns and villages. They suffered much from want, often being forced to satisfy their hunger on roots and leaves. One night St. Francis heard moaning and found one of the brothers dying of hunger. He rose and brought out food from his own scant supply, and forced him to eat.

The approval of the Pope opened the churches to their preaching, but they were too small. Even the Cathedral to which the Bishop invited him was insufficient for the crowds, and he was forced to resort

to the public squares. His words
were like a new revelation to his
hearers; they aroused men's con-
sciences, and touched their hearts.
They were not eloquent save with
the eloquence of a burning soul, filled
with sympathy and pity and love.
He saw that men were miserable
and longed to help them. The
whole community was moved; the
poor, because they felt that they
had found a friend, a brother, a
champion, one who knew their sufferings and could help them; the
rich, because they saw in him one
who lived above the level of their
lives, who was free from their sordid
ambitions, indifferent to the things
for which they were selling themselves. Civil dissensions had broken
out again in Assisi; the nobles and

the people were on the verge of war.
Through the influence of St. Francis
the trouble was averted, and har-
mony established; the nobles granted
a liberal charter in consideration of a
small annual payment, and the inhab-
itants of the villages were put on à
level with those in the city. Num-
bers were added to the order, mostly
young men, many of high rank, and
some of intellectual culture. It was
no light task to govern them in a life
of extraordinary self-denial and poverty, to keep them happy and efficient
in carrying out a social and religious
revolution, yet without monastic con-
veniences or the formality of a definite rule. His success is evidence
not only of his goodness, but of his
wisdom and common-sense.

The *Brothers Minor* was the name

that he gave to the order. One day one of the Brothers was reading to him the rules which he had drawn up for their guidance, and came to the words, "Let the Brothers, wherever they may find themselves called to labour or serve, never take an office which puts them over others; let them always be under, *sint minores*." The poor and the common people at that time were called *minores*, and the rich and powerful *majores*. Francis thought this was a providential intimation of the name to be given them, and he said: "Let them be called *Fratres Minores*"— the Brothers Minor; and by that name, or the Minorites, the order has been known through the world.

It was not a mendicant, but a labouring order which St. Francis

really founded. He insisted rigor-
ously on the duty of work; he was
inflexibly severe on idleness. Those
who entered the order were to continue their calling if they had one, if
not they were to learn one. He
himself worked as a wood carver.
They were to exchange the fruits of
their labour for the necessities of life,
but under no circumstances to receive
money; where they were unable to
get or to do sufficient work they were
not to be ashamed to ask for food.
Did not Jesus and his disciples live
on bread that was given them? But
work was to be the rule, begging the
exception. Evidently life at Portiuncula differed much from that of the
convent; it was more like a work-
shop than a monastery. Men entered it without a novitiate of any

kind; it was enough if they wanted to follow Christ, and were ready to show their sincerity by giving up all they possessed for the poor. So much youth, freedom, simplicity, love, drew the eyes of men toward it, and it increased rapidly.

Not only men but women were attracted by this desire of a nobler life. The first to come was a girl of noble rank named Clara Sciffi. She had heard St. Francis preaching in the Cathedral. His words appealed to her ardent, enthusiastic spirit. She determined to break away from an idle, luxurious life, to give herself to the service of God and the poor. On the night of Palm Sunday, 1212, she left her father's castle secretly, and came to St. Francis, offering herself to him. He recognised at once the sincerity of her heart; without test or novitiate he accepted her. He read to her the words of Jesus which were the rule of the order, received her vows of conformity, her hair was cut off, and she was taken to the house of the Benedictine nuns to remain for a time. The next morning her father came furiously upbraiding and abusing every one, but she was firm, and he was compelled to give up the idea of taking her away by force. St. Francis succeeded in obtaining from the Benedictine monks the little chapel of St. Damian, and here, where the words of Christ had first come to his own soul, a home was established. He took measures to prevent any but the most necessary communication between the two communities, and when

other houses arose placed them under
the care of the Church. They were
called *The Poor Clares* and grew
into a great order. For the rest of
his life in the Lady Clara he had
a kindred spirit, pure, brave, unsel-
fish, devoted to carrying out his idea.
In his hours of discouragement, she
comforted him, when he doubted
his mission and thought his work a
failure she strengthened him. Their
love for each other was full of tender
romance, but so pure and spiritual
that no breath of scandal has ever
been breathed upon it. She caught
the Franciscan spirit completely, its
brightness, its generosity, its strength,
its practical character. She survived
him twenty-seven years, and to the
day of her death struggled to carry
out his idea with a holy heroism that

makes her one of the loveliest pictures in religious history.

Others, both men and women, who were married and could not leave their homes, desired to share in the movement. They came from all quarters and classes imploring St. Francis in some way to help them to live better lives and to renounce the world. This led to the formation of a third order, the *Tertiaries*, as they were called. Francis no more condemned the family and property than Jesus did. He felt that he himself and his followers were exceptions. Their work was in a sense apostolic, and needed absolute freedom. He saw that this life was not possible or desirable for all. The Rule of the Tertiaries was simple and practical. It required the cultivation of a loving spirit, the simplest possible way of living, and the distribution to the poor of all that was not needed for the simplest wants. It forbade the use of arms except in defence of the Church and the country. To close the heart to hatred, and open it in love to the sick and the poor, was the main requirement of the new order. It was a religion of practical love instead of form. Its success was immediate, and its results a far-reaching revolution. The first thing that it did was to strike a mortal blow at the feudal system in Italy. The Tertiaries refused to take up arms for the feudal lords in their endless quarrels with one another. The Pope was appealed to. Honorius was then in the papal chair, a man who loved the poor and longed for peace. He took the side of the order, and forbade interference with them under penalty of excommunication. Military service was swept away and feudal oaths abolished. Again the nobility appealed to the Pope, and again he protected the order. Francis lived to see the feudal system broken throughout Italy.

Something of his own spirit permeated society; a vast body of men and women were roused to religious activity and the reality of the Christian life. The gulf between the rich and the poor was in a measure bridged, and a more humane spirit entered into all ranks. The poor felt that they were no longer outcasts from society when men cared for them and denied themselves for their help. The rich felt that the poor were their brothers when they recognised their duty and did it. The proletariat of the cities, spurned by the nobles and despised by the artisans, learned that Christianity could bring the fortunate and the unfortunate together, and consecrate the strong to the service of the weak. St. Francis saved society in his day by bringing the classes together in sympathy and binding them through duty. Civilisation received a new impulse as men ceased to strive for domination in perpetual warfare, and for years there was peace in Italy.

Thus in the short space of three years, from such a small beginning, the organisation developed into an immense society; with almost incredible rapidity it made itself felt throughout Italy, and soon throughout the world. The name of St. Francis became a household word among all ranks of men, and the whole country was moved with a desire for better things. To effect such a revolution required no common powers; it implies something more than a pious, loving, extravagant enthusiast. St. Francis was a born ruler and organiser of men, whose power was that of magnetic influence, resting upon high sanctity, with deep insight into character, far-reaching wisdom and common-sense, complete self-forgetfulness.

His efforts were not confined to his own country. He said once to Cardinal Ugolini. " Do you think God has raised up the Brotherhood for the sake of this country alone ? Verily I say unto you God has raised it up for the awakening and salvation of

all men, and shall turn souls not only
in the countries of those that believe,
but also in the midst of the infidels."
In the middle ages there were, broadly
speaking, but two callings or pro-
fessions for men, that of the soldier
and that of the priest or monk. St.
Francis combined the two, he was
both saint and soldier. He was still
a knight and retained the knightly
spirit. It was this, perhaps, which
gained for him in so great degree
the admiration and imitation of the
noblest spirits of his time. There
was in him that longing for the
unknown, that thirst for dangers,
adventures, sacrifices, which makes
the history of his century so attractive in spite of its dark features.

He believed that the Saracens
also would accept the Gospel if it

only could be presented to them, and he longed to be the messenger to carry to them the priceless blessing. In the autumn of 1212 he set out on this new kind of crusade, and sailed for Syria; but his ship was wrecked in a tempest and cast upon the coast of Slavonia, and he was compelled to return to Ancona. Prevented from reaching the infidels in Syria, he determined to seek them in Spain and Morocco. With Bernard Quintavalle, his first disciple, he sailed from Pisa and landed in Barcelona. It is uncertain how long he remained in Spain, but long enough to found several chapters. He was preparing to go across to Morocco, but the constant fatigue and exposure brought on a violent fever, which made the journey into Africa impossible.

St. Francis of Assisi

On his return to Italy he again visited Rome, and here for the first time he was brought into contact with another great soul of his time, Dominic, the founder of another great order, the Dominicans, destined to become the rivals and often the enemies of the Franciscans. The two men became warm friends, though widely differing in character. Dominic was a trained theologian, and the members of his order, equipped with all the learning of the day, skilled in debate, were especially intended to be a defence to the church against heretics. To Francis, scholastic learning was nothing; he regarded it as a foe to simplicity. Piety, not learning, was to him the one thing needful, and the poor, not heretics, the object of his preaching.

The Labours of an Apostle

Dominic aimed at teaching the dogmas of the Church; Francis, to show the world the beauty of holiness. The one has come down to us through the centuries as *The Hammer of God;* the other as *The Father of The Poor.*

It was not until six years later that St. Francis was able to fulfil his desire of going as a missionary to the Saracens. In June, 1219, he sailed from Ancona with a few companions for Egypt. The Bishop of Acre writes: "We saw Brother Francis arrive, who founded the Minorite Order. He is a simple man without letters, but very lovable, dear to God as well as to men. He came to us when the army was lying under Damietta." Francis was greatly distressed by the moral condition of the crusading forces, their disorganisation and want of discipline. He predicted a great defeat, and on August 29 they attacked the Saracens and were terribly routed. After preaching to the armies for a time he passed over to the camp of the infidels with a courage which was regarded as madness. He was seized and thrown into chains. Afterwards he was brought into the presence of the Sultan, a man as large and generous-minded as he was brave, who recognised in Francis a kindred spirit. He refused him permission to preach, but sent him back with presents. A number of legends have grown up in regard to the interview, how Francis challenged the priests of Mahomet to pass through the fire, how the Sultan endeavoured to con-

vert him, how at last he was condemned to death and the Sultan
privately interfered and released him.
We have no reliable foundation for
these stories.

Though the mission to the Saracens failed, it had great effect on
the crusaders, and many joined the
order. An eye-witness, Jacques
de Vitry writes: "Master Reynier,
Prior of St. Michael's has entered
the order of the Brothers Minor, an
order which is multiplying rapidly
on all sides because it imitates the
primitive Church, and follows the
life of the Apostles in everything.
The Master of these Brothers is
named Brother Francis. He is so
lovable that he is venerated by all.
After he came among us so great
was his zeal that he did not fear to

go to the army of our enemies, and preach the word of God to the Saracens. He had not much success, but on his departure the Sultan asked him in secret to show him by some miracle which was the best religion. Colin, the Englishman, our clerk, has entered the same order, as also two others of our companions, Michael, and Master Matthew, to whom I had given the rectorship of Sainte Chapelle. Cantor and Henry have done the same, and others whose names I forget."

The same year another mission was sent to Spain, which ended in tragedy and martyrdom. In Seville, a city then in the hands of the Saracens, the little band was seized and sentenced to death.

The Labours of an Apostle

The sentence was changed to banishment to Morocco. The Moors acted at first with great moderation and patience. They sent them out of the country under a guard that they might return to Europe. They escaped and went back to Morocco, where again they openly preached the Christian religion. Again they were thrown into prison, from which they were released under the royal command to leave the country. The command was disregarded, and this time the patience of the authorities seems to have been exhausted. They were tortured with savage cruelty, dragged through the streets, terribly beaten, rolled on sharp pieces of glass, and their wounds rubbed with acid to intensify their sufferings. The king

visited them in prison, and endeavoured to induce them to give up
their work. When all his efforts
were vain, in a fit of rage, he killed
them with his own hands.

Their martyrdom, and the mission
of St. Francis to the East, had an
effect that was felt far and wide.
The world could not but feel that
these men were in deep earnest.
The sight of them, many of them
cultured and high-born men, ex-
posing their lives with sublime
courage, and laying them down with
heroic fortitude to advance the
cause of the Cross, not by arms, but
by loving devotion, extending the
same self-sacrificing efforts to the
hated infidel, — such a sight sent
through Europe a thrill of admiration for those who could live and

die for their faith, with a charity toward all men, which nothing could check. Within ten years of its inception the Franciscan movement was no longer a power in Italy merely, but had become a force throughout the civilised world.

V

THE SUFFERING SERVANT

To have a true and high ideal, to feel in it the inspiration of God, to know that it has power to uplift the world; to give life and all to the service of it, and then to see it taken away, corrupted, debased, transformed from a power of freedom into a means of enslavement, and be powerless to help it, — that is the greatest sorrow a noble spirit can possibly know. That was the sorrow of St. Francis' closing years.

On his return from the East he found that changes had taken place.

Before setting out he had appointed
two men, the brothers Matteo, to be
vicars in his place. They began at
once to make innovations, to relax
the vow of poverty, and to multiply
observances, to make religion a
matter of rite and ceremonial, to
substitute bondage for freedom.
At Bologna he found that a monastery had been built and had become
the property of the Order. He com-
manded that it should at once be
given up, and even the sick should
be moved from it. The main dif-
ference between the Rule of St.
Francis and that of other orders
was in regard to the possession of
property. Other orders were under
the vow of poverty, but it applied
only to the individual members; the
order itself could hold possessions

and become rich. Francis had seen
the evil which resulted from this.
It was no madness or fanaticism,
but a far-reaching statesmanship, by
which he made it a characteristic
feature of his Rule that the possession of property, whether by the
individual members or the Order,
was absolutely forbidden. He saw
that if this principle were violated
the Brothers Minor would degener-
ate into one of a number of monastic
orders, whose members constituted a
kind of religious aristocracy, living
in ease and luxury and seclusion
from the service of the world.

As the Order grew some com-
plained because it was not like the
other orders, with fine abbeys and
large revenues. The authorities at
Rome were continually urging the

propriety of possessing religious houses and lands. A party sprang up within the Order which was continually pressing upon him the need of accepting that which he regarded, and rightly regarded, as the sequel shows, to be a snare of the devil. This prospect filled him with sorrow during the rest of his life. He knew what would happen, and what exactly did happen, if the order accepted gifts of lands and houses and estates; that poverty, self-sacrifice, humility, love, with their living, unanswerable appeal, would be chased away, and the power would be gone. This was the cross he had to bear, to see his beautiful vision realised only to be lost. In spite of the efforts of his biographers to throw a veil over it, his anguish constantly appears. " The time will come," he said once, " when our order will have so lost its good renown that the members will be ashamed to show themselves by daylight." Again, toward the end of his life, he said, " We must begin again to create a new family, which will not forget humility, which will go and tend the lepers as of old, which will, not only in word but in deed, set itself beneath its fellow creatures." His last will and testament is a most touching document. From the official lives it was always omitted, but in the recently discovered " Mirror of Perfection," written by Brother Leo within a year of the saint's death the mind of St. Francis is revealed to us, and the whole spirit of it is a kind of heart-breaking groan that his great ideal had been spoilt for him.

A dream that he once had came back to him, in which he had seen a little black hen, which in spite of her efforts was not able to spread her wings over her brood. The poor little hen was himself, and the chickens were the Brethren. About this time the Pope issued a bull commanding all who entered the Order to undergo a year's novitiate, none to leave it during life, and all wearing the habit to exercise implicit obedience to the Church. The strong hand was laid upon it, never to let go; the freedom and simplicity were forever gone. Henceforth it was impossible for St. Francis to remain at the head of it. Discouraged and heartsick, he felt that the administration of the Order needed a different character from himself. He was so submissive, so humble, so obedient that he never thought of asserting his own will against that of the Pope, the Vicar of Christ; but his vision became obscured, he began to waver and almost to doubt himself and his mission. Such doubts come to the noblest spirits in times of weakness and discouragement. He searched himself anxiously to see if there had not been some self-complacency in his work. He resolved to put the direction into the hands of another, and he chose Pietro di Catana. "From henceforth," he said to the Brothers, "I am dead to you, but here is Brother Peter, whom you and I will obey." The Brothers could not restrain their tears when they saw themselves become in some sort orphans, and Francis, raising his eyes and clasping his hands, prayed: "Lord, I return unto Thee this Thy family, confided unto me. Now, as thou knowest, most sweet Jesus, I have no longer strength nor ability to keep on caring for them. I confide them therefore to the ministers. May they be responsible before Thee at the Day of Judgment if any Brother by their neglect or bad example or by a too severe discipline ever wanders away." Pietro died a few months after, and Brother Elias became the vicar-general.

Elias was one of the very earliest members of the Brotherhood, a friend whom Francis loved and trusted with his whole heart. He seems to have been a man of high character and

great administrative ability, but also
of great ambition, not of a personal
kind, but for the future of the Order.
He had come to regard the idea of
Francis as impractical and impossible
for the guidance of a great organisation.   He cleverly contrived, without
openly violating the Rule, or oppos-
ing the wishes of Francis, to bring
about a very different condition of
affairs.   Italy and the other countries
were divided into provinces, each
having its own provincial officers.   It
was necessary that these officers
should have official residences and
subordinates, convents and churches,
and all the dignity of officials in other
orders.   The Brothers entered the
families of high personages of the
papal court, became their confidential
attendants, courtiers, intriguing for

the wealth and power of the Order.
The changes were made either without the knowledge or against the will
of Francis. His last years were a
perpetual protest against them, but
he had no power with which to op-
pose them save his teaching and example. This was consistent to the
end. One day he was the guest of
Cardinal Ugolini. When they were
about to sit down to dinner the other
guests were surprised to see him
come in with his hands full of pieces
of dry bread which he proceeded to
distribute to the noble company.
His host began to reproach him, but
Francis explained that he had no
right to forget for a sumptuous feast
the bread of charity on which he was
fed every day, and that he desired to
show his brethren that the richest

table was not worth so much to the poor in spirit as this table of the Lord.

But the end was drawing near. A life of such hardship and self-denial with such constant strain on mind and heart could not be a long life. *In mezzo del cammin di questa vita,* as Dante says, in the middle of the way of this life, when he was but forty-four years of age, he was called to his rest. He was preaching near Foligno, when in some way the warning came to him that the end was not far off. He retired with four of the Brothers to Verna, a rugged mountain peak near the borders of Tuscany, to prepare by prayer and meditation for death. They built there a little hut of boughs as in the old days. Here he was more than ever absorbed in the thought of the crucified Christ, the Man of sorrows. He grieved that he had not been found worthy of martyrdom, that he had not been able to give himself more completely for One who had completely given Himself for him. He often remained for many hours at the foot of the altar reading the Gospels, and the Book always opened of itself at the story of the Passion. On the night of Sept. 14, 1224, he spent the whole night in prayer, and in the morning he had a vision. He saw, so the story goes, a great light, and in the midst of the light a seraph nailed to a cross, who looked upon him with a look of tender love. He continued for a long time in a kind of trance of absorbed contemplation. When the vision faded he found on his body marks corresponding to the five wounds of our Lord, dark excrescences on his feet and hands like the heads of nails, and a red mark on his side, from which a little blood occasionally exuded.

It is a strange story, but not necessarily incredible. The domain of mental pathology is still largely an unexplored field. The influence of the mind upon the body is very imperfectly understood. In a single night men's hair has been known to turn gray under the influence of intense emotion. Physically it is not impossible that such constant concentration of mind on the subject of the Saviour's sufferings, with an intense desire to suffer for Him and with Him, may have had such an effect on his body. However the story may have been embellished by later legendary details, the weight of evidence is strongly in favour of it; it rests on contemporary testimony of the strongest kind. His three early biographers write of it with the precision of eye-witnesses. At the General Chapter at Geneva shortly after his death, one of his companions, when questioned by the general of the Order, said: "These sinful eyes have seen them, these sinful hands have touched them." The marks are said to have been seen by more than seven hundred persons. After weighing the probabilities against it, and the evidence for it, I am inclined personally to believe that something of the kind actually took place.

The Suffering Servant

After the vision of the *stigmata* Francis was affected with a disease that threatened him with blindness. He sought the aid of a physician at Rieti who was celebrated for his skill. According to the imperfect science of the time the remedies were very painful, consisting chiefly of bleeding and cauterising. A red-hot iron was drawn across his brow, and the inflammation encouraged and increased by continual incisions causing great suffering. Eager to continue his labours he preached whenever it was possible in the neighbouring districts, and made several missionary journeys. He was obliged to ride on an ass, for he was no longer able, as was always his custom, to travel on foot. Wherever he went the people received him with the utmost enthusiasm; he had completely gained their hearts. They believed in him and loved him. His sermons were necessarily short, but more impressive than ever, worn as he was with illness, emaciated, feeble, his voice weak, but his face more beautiful than ever in its extreme pallor, and its usual expression of strength and tenderness deepened by the marks of suffering.

Dropsy was now added to his other afflictions and the thin limbs were terribly swollen. He suffered also from hemorrhages reducing him to extreme prostration. St. Bonaventura writes: "He began to suffer from so many infirmities that there was scarcely one of his members but was tormented with incessant pain."

The Suffering Servant

He wanted to die at Assisi, with its many tender memories. The journey lay through Perugia, but they were afraid to take that way lest the citizens would compel him to remain, that the town might have the prestige of his death. By a circuitous way, under a strong escort, he reached Assisi at last. He was received with the subdued rejoicing of those who loved him, but knew they could not have him long. He was taken into the Bishop's palace, where he had every tender care. But the journey had been too much for him and he grew rapidly worse. Every movement was accompanied by intense pain, yet his sweet patience and cheerfulness never failed him. He always spoke of pain and death as his dear sisters, and he was always asking for singing to uplift his mind above his troubles. Greater than any suffering of body was his grief over the decadence and loss of purity in his Order, mingled with self-reproaches for his own cowardice. Why had he deserted his post and given up the direction of his family? "Where," he would cry, "are they who have ravished my brethren from me, who have stolen away my family?" Shattered as he was, he would try to rise from the bed saying: "Ah, if I could only go again to the Chapter General I would show what my will is."

Forgetful of his own sufferings he thought with divine sadness of humanity, for each member of which he would give his life, and he dictated a letter to all the members of the Order to be read at the opening of the Chapters : —

"To all the revered and well-beloved Brothers Minor, the oldest and the most recent, Brother Francis, a mean and perishing man, your little servant, gives greeting. God has sent you through all the world that by your words and example you may bear witness of Him, and that you may teach all men that he alone is all-powerful. Persevere in discipline and obedience, and with an honest and firm will keep that which you have promised. . . . Keep nothing for yourselves that He may receive you without reserve who has given Himself to you without reserve. Let us not be wise and learned according to the flesh, but simple, humble, and pure. We should never desire to be above others, but rather to be below, and to obey all men.

" To all Christians, monks, clerics, or laymen, whether men or women, to all who dwell in the whole world, Brother Francis, their most submissive servitor, presents his duty, and wishes the true peace of heaven, and sincere love of the Lord.

" Being the servitor of all men, I am bound to serve them and to dispense to them the wholesome words of my Master. This is why, seeing I am too weak and ill to visit each one of you in particular, I have resolved to send you my message by this letter, and to offer you the words of our Lord Jesus Christ, the Word of God, and of the Holy Spirit, which are spirit and life. . . .

" I, Brother Francis, your little

servitor, I beg and conjure you by
the love that is in God, ready to kiss
your feet, to receive with humility
and love these, and all other words of
our Lord Jesus Christ, and to con-
form your conduct to them. And
let those who receive them and
understand them pass them on to
others. And if they thus persevere
unto the end, may they be blessed
by the Father, the Son, and the Holy
Spirit. Amen."

Death was now near. He wanted
to be carried to Portiuncula, and to
die beside the humble chapel where
he had heard God's voice calling
him to his work. They carried him
down the hill in a litter. When
half-way they reached the hospital,
where long ago he had first tended
the lepers. He asked to be set down

on the ground with his face to Assisi, and raising his hand he bade farewell to his native place and blessed it. To be back once more at Portiuncula was a great joy to him. His last days were full of happiness. " He went to meet death singing," says Thomas of Celano.

He desired to see those whom he loved one by one, and to bless them. They knelt round his bed and his right hand rested on the head of Brother Elias. "Whom does my hand touch?" he asked, for the poor blind eyes could not see. They told him it was Elias. "That is well, my son, I bless thee in all and for all; I bless thee as much and more than I can ; may He who can do all supply what I cannot do. Farewell, dear sons, keep the fear of God, abide ever in Jesus Christ. Evil days draw on. You will pass through terrible trial. Many will fall away through scandals. Blessed are they who persevere. I go to God. I have served Him with all my soul. I leave this world in the fulness of trust. May His grace abide with you."

Just before his death a touching incident took place. He had never been ordained to the priesthood and he could not consecrate the Sacrament, but he sent for bread and blessed it, and gave a piece to each, and they ate together in memory of the body that was broken for them. Then he asked them to read to him once more the story of the Passion as written in St. John's Gospel, beginning with the words, "Now before the feast of the passover, when Jesus knew that his hour was come that he should depart out of this world, unto the Father, having loved his own which were in the world he loved them unto the end." On Saturday, Oct. 3, 1226, without struggle or sigh he entered into his rest.

He was buried in the little church of St. Mary of the Portiuncula, where two years later, Pope Gregory IX. came to lay the cornerstone of the great church erected to his memory. There are three churches one above another. In the crypt lies the body of the saint. In the middle building is intact the little church where he first heard the call of God, and which he repaired with his own hands. Close by the little church, under the dome of the great basilica, is the cabin in which he died, and just outside the wall is the cell in which he first lived. It is vast, gloomy, pretentious, oppressive, like a mausoleum of something that has died and vanished, seeming to tell how the great Roman system seized the beautiful ideal of St. Francis and pretending to admire it, appropriated, exploited, debased it, and then turned it to its own account, changing a great enthusiasm for men into a power of spiritual domination. As we look at the little chapel and cabin and cell, and then at the great church, rich, powerful, pretentious, we feel the immense gulf which separated the ideal of St. Francis from the Church that canonised him. Christ made the saint; the Church buried him.

VI

SUCCESS AND FAILURE

THE life of St. Francis is a great encouragement to our Christian faith. It is a manifestation of the power of Christ at work in the thirteenth century as well as in the first. It has been said "It takes a Jesus to forge a Jesus," meaning that the life and character of Christ are so far beyond human invention that, as Rousseau says, "the inventor would be a greater wonder than the hero." So it may be said that it takes a Christ to make a St. Francis. The reality and power of his life prove the

9   129

reality of the power behind it, and of that reality there is no reasonable room for doubt. The same process of historical criticism, which has established beyond sceptical denial the reality of the life of Christ, has established with something of the same certainty the reality of St. Francis' life. It was beyond the invention of the times. It was in opposition to all the ideals of the age. It was one long struggle with the Church, and not until the Church had spoiled his ideal and ruined his work did it consent to canonise him as a saint.

Where imagination and fiction have touched the life of Jesus it can easily be recognised, as in the Apocryphal Gospels. Imagination and fiction have also surrounded the life of St. Francis with the legendary and

the miraculous, but in the main the
fiction can easily be sifted from the
reality. That some things regarded
as miraculous occurred is not incredible, it is even probable. If his life
was the closest following of Christ
since the days of the Apostles it is not
surprising if something of the power
of Christ and the works of Christ was
manifest in him. If he fulfilled the
conditions of Christ's promises why
should it be incredible to Christians
that those promises were fulfilled in
him? But his miracles, like those of
Christ, were all works of love; the
greater part of them were the healing
of those nervous disorders and mal-
adies so common in his time. Some
of them are clearly legendary, but
some come to us on such high authority, and rest upon such strong evi-

dence as to carry with them at least a reasonable probability.

His character was so far in advance of his age, and even of our own age, that it cannot be in any great degree the work of invention. He is often thought of as a sweet, sympathetic, child-like character, lovable but visionary and unpractical. Such a view of him is quite insufficient. He was a man of keen intelligence strong intellectual powers, large common-sense. He was an enthusiast, but not unbalanced; intense, not narrow and pedantic; severe toward himself, always inclined to mitigate the severity of others. He said once: " We must use discretion in the treatment of our brother the body if we do desire to excite in us a tempest of sadness. Let us frankly remove from it any cause of complaint and then it will accept our vigils and lend itself to our prayers." Eccentricity and exaggeration for their own sake were hateful to him. He was absolutely sincere. No sort of pretence could find place in his strong, simple nature. If there was any exaggeration it was in the desire never to appear other than he actually was. Once when he was ill a Brother, seeing that in the cold of winter he had nothing on but a patched tunic, got a piece of fox-skin and brought it to him. "My father," he said, "you suffer from your liver and your stomach; let me sew this skin under your tunic." St. Francis answered: "I accept what you wish, but you must sew as large a piece outside, that the brethren may know that I allow myself this comfort."

St. Francis of Assisi

He was a man of great refinement, both of character and manner. He was no recluse, unacquainted with the evils of the world, but his delicate refinement of spirit enabled him to throw them off so that they did not enter his soul. His appearance and manners were those of a polished gentleman, and much of his extraordinary power came from his graceful and unfailing courtesy. St. Bonaventura speaks of his "exquisite sweetness, his perfect manner, his bright temper, his generosity which gave without ever counting the loss." Of more than medium height, his face was oval, his eyes dark and clear, his hair thick, his nose straight and delicate, his teeth white and equal, a black beard not thickly grown, square shoulders, small hands and feet.

There was about his whole person a charm and grace that made him exceedingly lovely. All these characteristics are found in the most ancient portraits.

He had an iron will, indomitable courage and constancy, combined with a wonderful meekness and humility. Men of strong will are often hard and masterful, but in St. Francis firmness was combined with sweetness; an inflexible purpose with great gentleness of execution; a high ideal with a large charity; a horror of sin with unfailing mercy for the sinner. His love for men knew no limits. In every one he saw one for whom Christ died, and for whom he was willing to die. There was nothing he was not willing to do for the weakest and the worst. To the sick and the sorrowful he was tender as a mother; but it was the poor who especially claimed his heart. In every poor man he saw an image of Christ, and a possible reflection of Christ. Everything that interested his fellow men interested him — the aspirations of the people, their struggles for freedom, their literature, their song, their amusements, the trials of their daily lives moved his ever ready sympathy. Perhaps no other man, unless it were St. Paul, ever had such a wide-reaching, all-embracing sympathy; and it may have been even wider than St. Paul's, for we have no evidence in him of a love for nature and for animals.

The love of St. Francis extended to all God's creatures. Brave as he was and prepared to endure any suf-

fering himself, he could not bear to
see dumb animals in pain. The
beasts, the birds, the flowers, the sun
and moon, he always spoke of as his
brothers and sisters. There is a
charming story of the swallows,
which is one of the most familiar
stories of his life. Once when he
was preaching he could not make
himself heard for the twittering of
the swallows about him, and turning
to them, he said, " It is my turn to
speak now, little sister swallows.
Hearken to the Word of God, and
be quiet till I have finished." Of
course the story goes on to say that
they were immediately still and lis-
tened with great attentiveness to his
sermon. Once he saw a rabbit
caught in a trap. "Come to me,
little brother," he said, and took it

in his arms and released it. At
Christmas he always wanted corn
spread in the lanes and the fields
that the cattle and the birds might
share in the Christmas joy. He
loved and cultivated flowers, and
wherever the Brothers found a resting place they were required to cul-
tivate a little place for flowers. This
feeling for nature and for animals
was much more unusual then than
it is now, and more unusual in the
Southern than in the Northern
nations.

Love to St. Francis was religion,
and religion was the expression of
love. His love found its inspiration
in the love of Christ, and extended
to everything that belonged to
Christ. For Christ himself that
love was beyond all words; it

filled all the capacities of his being. A deep, tender, personal devotion to the Crucified was the most characteristic feature of his life. He realised as few have done the meaning, the sorrow, the tender, awful solemnity of the Cross. In everything he saw Christ and loved Him. There was nothing forced or slavish in his imitation of Christ; it was the perfectly spontaneous outflow of his heart. His life was the response to the gracious call, "Follow me." St. Bonaventura says: "His heart was a perfect instrument tuned to the love of God. As soon as the words 'the love of God' touched it, as a violin responds to the bow, every chord within it vibrated." And again: "Jesus was all things to him; Jesus was on his lips, his eyes,

his ears, his hands, in his whole
being."

This was the source of his great
joy. There was nothing gloomy or
morose about his asceticism and
poverty. His religion was one of
joyousness. He had a horror of
sadness. He regarded mirth and
gladness as Christian duties. Never
was a soul more filled with penitential sorrow, but the sunshine of God's
love was always gleaming through it.
He was always breaking out into
song, especially the songs of the
Troubadours, which he never ceased
to love. Sometimes he would ac-
company himself on two sticks which
he used as an imaginary violin. He
saw, none more clearly, the darkness
the misery, the sin of the world; still
there was so much to be thankful

for, so much in men that he could admire and believe in, that he could not be sad. "My brother," he said to one of the Brothers who came to him with a gloomy face, "if thou hast some fault to mourn over, do it in thy cell, but here with thy brethren be as they are in countenance and tone." Nothing could empty his soul of its satisfaction in God. All life, all the world was but an opportunity to serve Him who was the joy of his life. Giving up all things, he gained all things; losing his life for Christ's sake, he found it.

The life of St. Francis is also a manifestation of the power of God working through man as well as in man; he is an example not only of what God can make of a sinful man like ourselves, but of what God can do through one who in complete self-surrender yields himself to the divine will. Mr. Moody, at the beginning of his career, was walking one day in Phœnix park, Dublin, and heard two men talking behind him. He did not know them, nor they him; it was a chance remark that fell from one of them. He said: "The world does not yet know what God can do through a fully consecrated man." It made a deep impression upon him and his whole life became an illustration of what God can do through a man truly consecrated to his service. St. Francis was a still more remarkable illustration of the same truth. Without learning or eloquence or wealth or rank he brought about one of the greatest religious revolutions and revivals that the world has ever known, and lifted the world a little nearer to God.

The monastic orders of his time were wealthy, aristocratic, cultured, exclusive, separate from the life of the people, shut up in convents, seeking their own spiritual welfare. St. Francis, filled with the love of Christ and following in the steps of Christ, went to the common people, who heard him gladly and received him with joy. He made religion popular, extending it beyond the confines of the cloister. In a day when to be religious meant to be a member of a monastic order, he brought home religion to the hearts of men and women in the world, and showed them that it was meant for them. He taught laymen that Christianity had a mission for them, especially to the poor. Matthew Arnold, a critic free from religious enthusiasm, says: "It was a profound instinct which enabled Francis more than any man since the primitive age to fit religion for popular use. He brought religion to the people. He founded the most popular body of ministers of religion that has ever existed in the Church. He transformed monachism by uprooting the stationary monk, delivering him from the bondage of property and sending him as a mendicant friar to be a stranger and sojourner, not in the wilderness, but in the most crowded haunts of men, to console them and do them good."

And Machiavelli, astute, cynical, worldly, declares in one of his discourses that Christianity would have been almost extinct " if Francis and Dominic had not renewed it and replaced it in the hearts of men by poverty and the example of Jesus Christ."

The friars in the early years of the Order were unlettered, simple-minded men, full of enthusiasm and self-sacrifice, popular preachers, exhorting men to follow Christ, and themselves practising what they preached. They spread rapidly throughout Christendom. In 1224, two years before the death of Francis, they landed in England, a little band of nine persons. Dr. Jessup, in *The Coming of the Friars*, describes their beginnings: " Outside the city walls of Lynn, York, Bristol, in a filthy swamp at Norwich, in a mere barn-like structure with walls of mud at

Shrewsbury, in 'Stinking Lane' at London, the Minorites took up their abode, and there they lived on charity, doing for the lowest the most menial offices, speaking to the poorest the words of hope, preaching to learned and simple such sermons — short, homely, fervent, emotional — as the world had not heard for many a day." Within five years of their landing they had houses in all the chief towns of England. In 1264 they are said to have possessed eight thousand cloisters and two hundred thousand members.

Their work was not confined to Christendom; it extended over the world. As early as 1258 a bull of Alexander IV. is addressed to the friars among the Saracens, Pagans, Greeks, Bulgarians, Cumans, Ethiopians, Syrians, Iberians, Alans, Cathari, Goths, Zichori, Russians, Jacobites, Nubians, Nestorians, Georgians, Armenians, Indians, Muscovites, Tartars, Hungarians, also those labouring among the Christians captured by the Turks. This is not a geographical enumeration, but a witness to the great zeal of the order. In 1289 two of them in China had built a Church at Pekin with a dome and bells: they had one hundred and fifty boys in their school and five thousand converts. They aided Columbus in preparing his expedition, and at Hayti the Franciscans opened the first church for religious service in the New World.

If the followers of St. Francis had been true to his ideal and instructions, they might have saved the world.

In so far as they were true they gave to religion a new momentum which lasted for more than a century and which has never been wholly lost. The rock of shipwreck was the possession of property. With divine wisdom St. Francis warned his disciples, as Christ also had done, of the evils and dangers of riches, of the power and advantages of poverty. Experience vindicated his teaching. The primitive Church in its poverty conquered the world; in its alliance with wealth it succumbed to the world. The same was true of the Franciscan movement. As early as 1230 some in the Order sought from the Pope an interpretation of the Rule of Francis. Gregory IX. issued a bill declaring that St. Francis could not bind his successors; that the agents of the Order could receive money and hold property for the use of the Brotherhood. This decision was marked by a relaxation in the vow of poverty and the beginning of a decadence in character and power. The duties that had been rendered for love were now performed for money, and money became the ruling passion. The friars were not only permitted to preach but to hear confession, to baptise, to bury, to grant indulgences; everything had its price and had to be paid for. In 1257 St. Bonaventura, then General of the Order laments that the Brotherhood had become an object of popular dislike on account of its greed, idleness, worldliness, and scandalous conduct.

The love of money proved indeed

"the root of all evil," and covetous-
ness opened the door to lust. The
darkest page in the story of the
friars is their licentiousness. Bonaventura in his many warnings shows
the extent and gravity of the evil.
Erasmus says: "They demand admission into private houses, they
come and go as they please, and the
owner does not dare refuse. Men
must take a stranger into their families, and the secrets of the household
are exposed to the world. Wise
men know that in such a multitude
all are not pure, and that monks are
made of flesh as other men."

All were certainly not pure, but all
were not faithless. During the hor-
rors of the Black Death in Europe
none were so devoted as the friars,
everywhere acting as ministers of

mercy while the parish priests fled from their posts. Not less than 150,000 of them perished in their zeal for the sick and dying. Two centuries later in the plague of 1528 the Franciscans showed that they had not forgotten the traditions of their Order; and in every age, while many have soiled its fame by their sin, some have proved themselves worthy of their founder.

It was a great idea, one of the divinest ever cherished in a human soul, beautifully embodied in St. Francis, but too high, too pure, too heavenly for those who came after him. It failed, and yet it did not wholly fail. The world was not saved by it, but the world was the better for it, and has never quite gone back to the conditions which prevailed before St. Francis came. No high ideal, no true and noble life, no faithful work for God has ever failed. The outward results may not have been permanent, but the inspiration has never been wholly lost. For seven hundred years, notwithstanding the failure of his followers, the life of St. Francis has been a power for good in the world, and Christ has seemed nearer, His example more possible, His teachings more practicable, because of this life which is but a far-off echo, a poor blurred copy of the one perfect life on earth.

Its inspiration has not yet been lost. On the contrary, after seven hundred years it is growing stronger. The day will come — it is nearer than we think — when the seed sown so long ago will bear new fruit, and some soul quickened by his example, strengthened by his spirit, will rise up in his likeness, and avoiding his mistakes, will take Christ at his word, will let Christ do with him what He will and carry him where He would have him go, in whom and through whom Christ will manifest His power in the twentieth as in the thirteenth century. He will stir society to its depths. The noblest spirits who are looking for their true leader will leap forward to follow him. A new order of Brothers Minor will gather about him. They will have no name, they will wear no garb, they will bear no badge, but they will be clothed with the ornament of a meek and quiet spirit. They will have no Prior or Vicar General, but will be directly under the Rule of Christ. " For one is your Master, and all ye are brethren." They will reverence the Church and be loyal to the Church, but they will not be in bondage to any great ecclesiastical organisation. They will be Brothers Minor, not in name but in spirit, regarding themselves as "less than the least of all saints," ignoring the endless social distinctions that separate men, not striving for the highest places in the social scale, but taking the lowest room, anxious to serve rather than to rule. "For I am among you as he that serveth."

They will regard their possessions, whether great or small, whether property or personal gifts, as belonging not to themselves, but to God, intrusted to them to use for Him.

Success and Failure

They will not wildly distribute their
goods to the poor, nor give up their
property to other men, but keep it
for God. They will not speak so
much of giving as of using. It is
always easier to give up than to use
wisely and well. When the rich
man comes to join the Order it
will not be said to him: "Go sell
all that thou hast and give to the
poor," but that which is still harder:
"Keep all thou hast for God, and
use it all for Him." When the
scholar comes he will not be told
that books are worthless and knowledge is nothing, but to get all the
knowledge that he can, to enrich his
mind and increase his power, that
he may have the more to give to
God and to use in the service of
men. When the politician comes

155

he will not be asked to leave his place and go about preaching the Gospel, but to use his political influence, his knowledge of social conditions, his power in the community only for the good of men. And women will not be required to turn their backs on society and shut themselves up like St. Clara and the poor Clares, but to use all their womanly power and influence for the purifying and elevating of society.

It will be an Order of *personal service;* each will use his gifts and opportunities himself, not by deputy or minister through Church or charity organisation. The essence of St. Francis' Rule was that it was personal. The lepers were to be tended by their own hands, the poor served, the Gospel preached, the life lived,

by themselves, not by some one else.
The weakness of our Christian service to-day is, that in the multiplicity
of organisations the power of person-
ality is largely lost; it is not the hand
that helps, but the machine; and the
giving of money, which is easy, takes
the place of personal service, which
is difficult.

It will be a great Order, not in a
mediæval but a spiritual sense; a
great Order of spiritual men and
women consecrated to God, following
in the steps of Christ, spreading
through all ranks of society from the
top to the bottom, and in every
operation of social life breathing the
spirit of faith and hope and love. Its
inspiration will be the love of Christ,
its glory the Cross of Christ, its ambition to bear that Cross and to

manifest that love throughout the whole world. And it will not fail. *Stat crux dum volvitur orbis.* While the cross stands those who embrace it in the arms of their faith and love will not fail nor fall. The Brothers Minor will be the Brethren of the Lord. " For whosoever shall do the will of God, the same is my brother and my sister and mother."

CPSIA information can be obtained at www.ICGtesting.com
Printed in the USA
LVOW122054220112

265030LV00011B/105/P